Critical Thinking:

How to Improve Your Critical Thinking and Problem-Solving Skills and Avoid the 25 Cognitive Biases in Decision-Making

Contents

INTRODUCTION 1

CHAPTER 1: WHAT IS CRITICAL THINKING? 3

How Do You Identify Whether Or Not You Are A Good Critical
Thinker? 4

Thinking Critically About Critical Thinking 4

The Process 6

Helping Your Child Think Critically 13

Fighting Biases 14

CHAPTER 2: GROUPTHINK 17

Groupthink? 17

Escaping Groupthink 18

CHAPTER 3: 25 COGNITIVE BIASES 22

CHAPTER 4: CONVERGENT AND DIVERGENT THINKING 46

Convergent Thinking 46

Divergent Thinking 47

CHAPTER 5: WHAT LAWYERS CAN TEACH YOU ABOUT LEARNING
HOW TO THINK 51

Thinking Critically in Your Career 57

CHAPTER 6: WAYS TO THINK MORE CRITICALLY 59

CONCLUSION 61

Introduction

Critical thinking is always going to be important. By being a good critical thinker and mastering the skills you will learn as you read, you will become a more active learner and be in control of how much information you absorb. This is an essential skill for students in all different fields. You will also become more empathetic because you will grow to understand all different viewpoints and backgrounds.

By acquiring the information provided in this book, you will become more creative, a better presenter, and more successful at self-reflection. This guide will offer you insights into how to think critically and solve problems quickly.

Critical thinking is a skill that will take you places. This book might help you get an A in your Advanced American History class or find a job at a law firm – no matter the context, the content is suitable for all ages. Learning how to think critically will help you make good choices and will allow you to be more confident in your decision-making. Critical thinking is necessary to be successful in many careers, and developing this skill now will only help you in your future endeavors. You will also be able to refer back to this if you have trouble remembering the process as it is simplistically outlined for you.

The following chapters will break down what critical thinking means and what you must have to achieve it. This guide will provide you with diagrams and explanations that will appeal to all different types of learners. The qualities of a critical thinker will be discussed along with an explanation of Groupthink. After understanding Groupthink, you will learn a few strategies to combat Groupthink from the standpoint of a leader and a group member. You will learn how to eliminate bias in your everyday life to become an efficient problem solver. This will also help you understand where biases are present in your life. This guide utilizes real-life examples which will allow you to relate to the content. There will also be interactive portions where you will be able to test your skills and apply what you have learned to examples.

Next, you will learn how to apply critical thinking skills to writing. This is very important when writing papers and analytical articles and can be helpful when completing a thesis for a degree. Writing critically is a rigorous process. It requires time and preparation; however, it is all worth it in the long run. This chapter on critical writing will allow you to write a clear, well-thought-out argument. You will also learn a few ways to determine what evidence to use. This section can be found in the chapter with cognitive biases because the cognitive biases can affect your writing.

This book will further teach you how to train your brain to react to different situations, first by allowing you to understand how your brain functions. This will be applied in the chapter containing Charles Munger's cognitive biases. You will also be told how to use questions to answer questions, which is another step in improving your ability to solve problems. These steps can later be referred to as a guide to breaking down difficult questions.

Next, convergent and divergent thinking will be discussed. You will learn what each is, where it can be used, and how to improve them in a brief chapter.

Lastly, you will learn a few strategies to increase how much you think critically in your everyday life.

Chapter 1: What Is Critical Thinking?

Previously, the need for critical thinking was discussed. However, you may still be wondering what critical thinking is and why it is important.

People often refer to critical thinking as a higher-order thinking or complex thinking. It is defined as the ability to analyze a situation objectively to formulate a judgment. Often, college professors have a hard time encouraging their students to utilize critical thinking because of the thought required to evaluate a situation and understand it thoroughly. This is due to laziness rather than an inability to perform the task of thinking critically. Thinking critically requires more thought than a simple recitation of a question and answer. The definition mentioned above refers to objective observation. This is similar to reading a book in the third person; you are able to see the plot unfold from the viewpoints of several different characters which may allow you to make more accurate predictions about future scenes in the book. This is a good way of looking at and understanding critical thinking.

Another important part of critical thinking is being able to take in the entirety of a situation and form your own thoughts or conclusions about what is happening. This may sound like it eliminates the objectiveness, but when accurately interpreting *all* of the evidence that has been gathered, you will be able to form clear, correct thoughts. This will allow you to make decisions more easily in tough situations where acting quickly is critical. It is also effective in eliminating bias. Acquiring both sides of the story always makes it easier for you to form your own opinion about something. This will also allow you to become a more efficient debater.

How Do You Identify Whether or Not You Are a Good Critical Thinker?

Critical thinking is a trait valued by many employers, and it is likely that they will test your critical thinking skills during the interview process. However, if this trait was not tested for, your work will show how good of a thinker you are. A weak critical thinker will begin to make costly errors. These mistakes will be repeated, which shows a lack of learning and a weak thinker will be unable to determine where action is necessary. These people will make assumptions, and the majority of their assumptions will be incorrect. This list continues to grow as better ways to evaluate a critical thinker are developed.

Thinking Critically About Critical Thinking

We use critical thinking to understand things, and this way of applied learning can further ingrain something in your mind. So let's break it down.

How to identify critical thinking:

▪ First, there has to be a question. It doesn't have to be impossible to answer, but it should be more complex than "What color is that car?" or "Where did you get your shirt?". Often, good questions include a political issue, but you would also use critical thinking to determine where your next move should be or what you should major in.

▪ Second, you have to examine evidence. This won't involve pulling fingerprints or examining blood splatter samples, but you want to look at the big picture. Take on that omniscient point of view that was mentioned earlier.

▪ Third, analyze any assumptions or biases. How does that work? Say you are talking to your friend about how her boyfriend treated her. She is upset; therefore, you can assume that she may not necessarily lay any fault in herself or she may exaggerate the situation. It's important to comfort your friend, but from a critical thinker's standpoint, you would want to consider this bias or even get the story from the boyfriend's point of view.

▪ Fourth, remove your emotions from the situation. Like in the previous example, your friend is unable to properly evaluate the situation because she is upset and emotionally involved. This is why it is smart to go to other people for advice about big decisions. Emotions clutter and often take over the mind because, of course, we are all only human.

o We can tie metacognition into this characteristic. Metacognition is thinking about your own thoughts. The act of removing yourself from a situation would require metacognition.

▪ Fifth, when you think critically, you want to consider other interpretations. So let's talk about things from the boyfriend's point of view. Maybe what offended your friend was not intended by her boyfriend, and thus miscommunication caused the argument. This is something you should consider when trying to seriously guide your friend through this difficult time.

▪ Sixth, sometimes, even after considering all of the information you possibly can, there are still some questions left unanswered – that's okay! Though you would like to know everything, sometimes every bit of information is hard to find. This is known as ambiguity, and to think critically, you don't need to eliminate it, but you do need to consider it.

o Sometimes, what you do not know is important when it comes to decision-making. When thinking critically, you must determine the ambiguity to determine whether you even have enough information to make a clear, rational decision about a topic. If you have not gathered enough information, go back to the drawing board to figure things out.

The Process

Depending on where you look, you can find critical thinking pictured in several ways depending on the diagram. An online image search brings up pyramids and many different flow charts documenting the critical thinking process.

The following is easy to explain and easy to understand based on the steps provided:

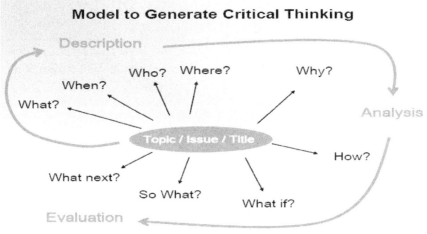

John Hilsdon, Learning Development Advisor, University of Plymouth

In the light gray, we see three steps that we will refer to as big picture steps. These are broad and will be broken down into more narrow topics. As you become better at thinking critically, you will be able to develop big picture steps more efficiently.

The first big-picture step is the description. You could also refer to this as an observation. This would be the first impression and then a complete breakdown of the evidence.

During this stage, you should be asking and answering almost all of the following questions:

- What? This will be a brief description of the event.
- When? At what time did the event take place? This will have significance in problem-solving.
- Who? There are many different "who's". Who was there? Who did it? Who knows about it? Who was there before? Who was there after?
- Where? What was the setting during the beginning, middle, and end?
- Why? What happened that prompted this event to take place? Why were all of the people there? Why did certain people leave?

It is also likely that they will be answered in the same order. Once you begin asking "why", you are making a transition from observation to analysis. During the analysis portion of critical thinking, you are using the answers to questions that were answered during the observation to make connections and answer more complex questions.

This is where you have to use your brain power to answer questions like:

- How did this happen?
- Will this happen again?
- What if it happens again?
- Why does this matter?
- What are our next steps to solving this problem?

Once you begin answering these questions, you will be more involved in the problem. There is a gradual increase in the amount of thought to answer each question. This is because, from the start of the process, the questions will be answered by others. However, as you dive deeper into the critical thinking process, you will be developing your own answers to the questions.

Evaluation is the third big-picture step. This is where you will begin forming your own opinions and answering the questions. You will even be able to ask your own questions at this point. This process is most apparent and utilized when solving a crime. If you are ever watching a crime show on television, try to identify when the investigators take each of these steps.

Please note that these questions are the minimum amount of questions. In a future chapter, using questions to answer questions will be discussed, but this is a good place for you to start problem-solving.

So now that we know what critical thinking is made of, what is a critical thinker made of?

A good critical thinker will have any number of the following characteristics:

• Be open-minded. If you have preconceived notions, you are getting involved in the situation instead of removing yourself from it.

• Be fair. Letting everyone get a chance to explain themselves is an integral part of critical thinking and coming to a correct conclusion. This definitely comes into play when working in a group and is important to keep in mind.

• Be skeptical. Don't believe everything you hear even if you should consider everything you hear. Remember, seeing is believing in many cases.

• Be reasonable. Listening to reasons is vital. Reasons will draw you away from emotion. Where reason leads you, you should follow. Even if this means admitting fault or changing sides.

Developing Your Critical Thinking Skills In 7 Stages

You may not start at stage one of this process, but if you recognize the stages, you can end at stage 6 in the process and become an effective critical thinker. We will also discuss strategies to improve your critical thinking that will push you to the highest stage possible.

At **Stage 1,** you pretty much have no idea what critical thinking is, and you don't know that there is a problem with your thinking. You are probably not the best at applied science or writing papers that require you to draw complex conclusions. You also lack self-awareness. To move to stage 2, you must acknowledge that you lack critical thinking qualities and decide to take action. At this stage, you are known as "the unreflective thinker".

At **Stage 2,** the thinkers are called "the challenged thinkers". This is when we become aware of our problems in our thinking. There is not a big jump between stages 1 and 2. You will still have a hard time answering complex application questions. However, you will have to begin using the suggested strategies to improve your thinking.

The "beginning thinker" is the **Stage 3** thinker. In this case, you are trying to improve but not making enough time to improve. It is possible to plateau at this point, and you will have a difficult time escaping this stage if you do not actively try to improve.

You will begin practicing in **Stage 4.** This is why you are known as the "practicing thinker". Now you will see greater increases in improvement over a short period of time. The brain is now learning and retaining the information you are feeding it. Practice is important because you are training your brain to do something. Eventually, your brain will react to critical thinking with muscle memory.

Stage 5 is when you become an "advanced thinker". You are pretty darn good at thinking, but you could be better. You still need to practice, and the more you practice, the better you will get.

Once you reach **Stage 6,** congratulations are in order. You are now a master thinker! Critical thinking is now second nature. Keep practicing and applying it to your daily life because the longer your brain goes without practice, the sooner you will forget!

How do you reach Stage 6? Don't worry; these stages come with strategies!

1. Use your wasted time

If you are truly committed, spend time during commercial breaks problem-solving. Even if you're not very good at first, don't be discouraged. The more you try, the better you will get. It can be practical too – think about your day. What went wrong? What went right? What can I do better next time? All of this will improve your thinking skills, and maybe they will even improve tomorrow. Don't forget to take notes!

2. A problem a day

This doesn't have to be a serious problem. This is about learning how to strategize and will help you with goal-setting. Let's say you have been thinking about buying a new couch. Think about all of the questions that will need answering when the time comes. What will I do with my old couch? Where will I buy my new couch? How much money do I need to save? Thinking this way will help you advance your life in ways you've never realized.

3. Improve intellectual awareness

INTELLECTUAL STANDARDS:
THINKING ABOUT MY THINKING

Clarity	To what extent is my point easily understood by myself and others?
Accuracy	To what extent is my information at hand true or correct without distortion?
Precision	To what extent is my information exact and specific to the necessary level of detail?
Relevance	To what extent does my information and input relate to the issue at hand?
Depth	To what extent am I engaging with the complexities of the issue?
Breadth	To what extent am I considering the issue at hand within the necessary contexts and relationships?
Logic	To what extent do my conclusions follow from the evidence?
Significance	To what extent can I identify and focus on the most important aspects of the issue at hand?
Fairness	To what extent am I able to avoid privileging my own biases?

Poster brought to you by i2a louisville.edu/ideas2action
Adapted with permission from The Miniature Guide to Critical Thinking Concepts and Tools by Richard Paul and Linda Elder. 2013. Tomales, CA. Foundation for Critical Thinking Press. www.criticalthinking.org

UNIVERSITY OF
LOUISVILLE.

There are universal intellectual standards. These include, but are not limited to, clarity, accuracy, precision, logicalness, and relevance. Define these terms for yourself and then decide how to improve them. If you are trying to improve clarity, focus on how well you communicate with people for a week then choose another standard to work on. Little things like these can go a long way.

The chart included above is from the University of Louisville, and it provides questions regarding intellectual standards. By using the chart, you will be able to identify the intellectual standards in your own life. You will also be able to enhance your intellectual standards which are important when attempting to reach Step 6.

4. Keep an intellectual journal

You are doing all of this work, so document it! Tracking how well you improve is a great motivator. It is also important to write things down because the saying "out of sight, out of mind" is so true. You can format your journal in any way that you want. Just make it easy to read, and use dates so you can track your progress over time.

5. Reshape your character

Everyone should have a goal of becoming a better person. You can choose one thing you don't like about yourself and try to improve it. Use your journal to write down specific interactions where you didn't like the way you reacted and reflect on it.

6. Deal with egocentrism

You are not more important than those around you. Don't act like it. This is a natural bias that affects everyone. However, you should try to limit it. That's not to say you should refrain from defending yourself in all instances. Instead, you should try to think logically and try to react the same way a rational person would.

7. Redefine the way you see things

Expand your knowledge. Read the news and talk to all different types of people. Listen to different viewpoints. Always open yourself to learning to become a more well-rounded individual. Having more knowledge will always be more beneficial than being ignorant. Remember that although you may define a situation one way, someone else will almost certainly define it in another way.

8. Understand your emotions

Any time you feel negatively about something, work your hardest to determine what exactly ignited such a reaction. The purpose of this is to gain more self-control. Try to consider the situation from different angles to diffuse the situation.

9. Think about who you are hanging out with

Who you spend time with influences your thoughts and actions. This is the reason we see different groups form in schools. This is also the reason we see labels develop, even though they are not necessary. Hang out with people who are going to lift you up and offer you good things. Remember, the size of your group is not what matters, but the quality of the people in it.

These strategies are just helpful tidbits to improve your critical thinking. This can be especially helpful if you are a rising college student or an adult looking to refresh your skills.

We've already discussed why critical thinking is important, and you probably know it is important if you chose this book to read. It is also important to know that you do not have to use all of these strategies every day. We all have something going on, and this may not be at the top of your list, but putting in an effort matters. If you see improvements in your life, share this with others. Having a world filled with critical thinkers will only improve our overall intelligence and the quality of living.

Helping Your Child Think Critically

It is easier to learn things when you are younger because many habits have not yet been formed. When you are an adult learning how to think critically, you have already spent so long thinking more simplistically that you will really have to try to think critically. For children, even toddlers, this will be a beneficial skill to learn.

You can add critical thinking to playtime. For example, when they get a new toy, instead of showing them how everything works and where the buttons that make it light up are, give them time to figure it out. At first, they will probably throw it or bang it on the floor or even take a taste test. This is okay – it is their way of learning. Once they are done with their initial evaluations, either they will give up on it and go play with a toy they know how to use, or they'll continue to investigate.

If they keep investigating, that is awesome. Their little gears are turning up there! If not, give them a nudge, give the toy back to them and ask suggestive, open-ended questions like "What is that?" or "What does this one do?". It is likely that they will respond positively to your questions. If you are excited about this new toy, they'll be excited about the new toy.

If you have asked all of the questions and given them a little more time and they are still not all the way there, now you can give them a nudge in the right direction. Now you are going to ask questions that will help them hypothesize – obviously they won't know these complex terms, but the learning process is still the same. Ask them things like "If we touch this, what will happen?". This could prompt them to press buttons or turn knobs.

You can also encourage them to think critically by talking about what you are doing. If you're playing with a light up toy, say "Let's press the button" before you press the button. Verbalizing your thought process can trigger their thought process in the same way.

It will be a very rewarding moment when your child is happy because they figured it out on their own. Their successes will make them more confident and motivated to find out how the next toy works.

Fighting Biases

Recognizing your viewpoint is as important as recognizing the viewpoints of others. This allows you to understand and limit biases. First, you should understand how to find these varying points of view. Talking to people is also useful; politics is a difficult topic to discuss, and a lot of people shy away from it when it's brought up. But if you truly want to eliminate bias, you should at least do your research.

We all know that interaction over the Internet is a million times easier than face-to-face interaction. This is detrimental in some ways, but it makes learning easier. Doing research is another way to identify different viewpoints. So many people blog nowadays, and I know that when I peruse my Facebook feed, I come across so many different opinions, even if I didn't ask. If you hear something you have never heard about before, look it up. We have so much knowledge at our fingertips.

As an avid reader, I have found that you can even find different viewpoints through fiction reading. Lots of authors today are ahead of the times, and their work is not only enjoyable but also full of information. Look at advertisements and see if you can identify whether they are leaning one way or another. Then research it. Don't limit yourself by being ignorant. Being knowledgeable is the best way to fight biases.

Bias is very apparent in everyday life, whether it is directed toward big picture things, such as the daily roles of men and women, or affording certain licenses toward people because they are famous or attractive. To think critically, you must recognize the presence of bias and eliminate it.

Being biased can be a sign that you are too close-minded or one-sided. To eliminate bias, you must practice what was outlined above. You can see that many of the things on the path to critical thinking are intertwined. Being open-minded and fair were two of the characteristics of a good critical thinker. These things will also help control and eliminate biases in a situation. A lot of the time, bias can be eliminated by removing yourself from a situation or understanding the other side's point of view. That being said, you don't necessarily have to be opinion-less in this situation. You want to make an educated decision about which side of an argument you choose to eliminate bias. By being educated, you are not being one-sided because you evaluated all positions being taken which is open-mindedness.

3 Biases That Directly Affect Critical Thinking

There are different levels of consciousness; therefore, there can be different levels of bias. Recognizing how this affects our ability to think critically is important.

These are four common biases that can be taken out of the picture once you are aware of them:

1. *Action bias*: think before you act! Critical thinking flies right out the window when you act before properly evaluating a situation.
2. *Confirmation bias:* you are not always going to be right. Lots of times, you will want to take the path that will confirm what you already know. Don't – humans aren't perfect! You are not always going to be right! So while you are looking for evidence that

supports your viewpoint, don't disregard the information that discredits your viewpoint. Often at times in a debate, the opposing viewpoint should be acknowledged to strengthen your argument anyway.

3. *Association bias*: this can be avoided by identifying correlation versus causation. This ties into a lot of superstitious beliefs – not washing your uniform before a game and believing something bad happened on Friday the 13th because it is a day of bad luck are a couple of examples. Recognizing the difference between a coincidence and two things that are actually related will help eliminate association biases.

Chapter 2: Groupthink

Groupthink?

If you have ever taken a psychology course, you've probably come across this term. If not, never fear; you will find all of the answers here!

By breaking down the word, you can probably piece together its meaning. Basically, Groupthink occurs when the members of a group make a decision that is not the best because nobody in the group wants to cause an issue by disagreeing. This type of thinking discourages individuality and creativity, and it may decrease your ability to solve a problem. There is also a term known as 'happy think'. At times, a leader of a group will encourage 'happy think' to lead outsiders to believe things are going well when there is no real progress being made.

If you are a manager or a boss, you should definitely be aware of how the workplace is affected by Groupthink. People coming to an agreement is not always a good thing. For example, what if every employee just decided they hated the management staff. You must be aware of this occurrence and take the necessary steps to create a better environment.

Escaping Groupthink

Fear of judgment is common, and people can be harsh. However, if we always agreed with everything we were told – or stayed quiet when we disagreed – nothing would ever change. This doesn't have to include anything monumental like women's rights. It can be small things, like the size of the font on your trifold for your group's English presentation. After all, appearance and readability can affect your grade. However, the point of being in a group is so that great minds can come together and create wonderful things. To do this, you must combat Groupthink, and rather than using the same opinions to create harmony, use different opinions to create a medley.

So now that we know that we *should* do it, how do we actually avoid Groupthink?

Instead of an established leader voicing all of their opinions to a group, everyone should form their own opinions and then come together to share and discuss the conclusions that have been developed.

Assigning roles can help too. Perhaps the leader could determine several different viewpoints and have each person research a specific viewpoint. This way, there will be evidence from all viewpoints and an educated decision can be made.

This can be compared to a play. Even if you don't physically act it out, the roles will probably follow something similar to a script.

Be open-minded! Don't discount someone's opinion because it opposes evidence. Use evidence to understand the pros and cons of an argument. This is an important part of all teams. There are not going to be any clones in a group. All of you will have separate thoughts. Don't be surprised when someone's opinion opposes yours – embrace it!

All in all, you can look at Groupthink and critical thinking as opposites. A lot of the critical thinking characteristics that we discussed previously should be utilized to avoid the negative effects of Groupthink. Working as a team can be extraordinary, and we don't want to discourage anyone from group work, but you should eliminate negativity and put-downs to have an effective group. All opinions should be considered and only be discounted when proper research has been done.

Don't avoid difficult topics. We all know it rains sometimes. Nothing is perfect. Don't pretend it is. The best way to get to the root of an issue is to face it head-on. It doesn't matter whether or not someone thinks you are too blunt. By eliminating fluff, it will be easier to solve the problem at hand. This can also be tied to happy think.

Let's look at a real-life situation to identify Groupthink. In this exercise, I will show you two examples, and I would like you to identify which is Groupthink and which is critical thinking using the definitions and characteristics outlined above. By seeing this real-life situation, it will be easier to identify when each is present in your own life. After each example is given, they will be broken down.

Example 1:

Julie's internship at the Northfolk Marketing Firm involves a lot of answering phones and getting paperwork. However, on Thursday, her boss approached her and offered her an opportunity to work on a project for Williams Architecture. They were seeking an advertisement that would be interactive and engaging. They were looking to attract new customers. Julie is inserted into one of the marketing groups. She feels like an outsider, and although this is an opportunity for her to shine, she is also afraid that she will not have an opportunity like this again if she shares her opinions and they are disregarded. During the meeting, her boss goes over all of the usual advertising techniques – billboards and radio ads – but nothing seems to be out of the box. Julie doesn't believe she has any true ideas to add, so she decides not to mention it. Even the senior marketers are going right along with her boss; so why would she . oppose?

While this example is simple, you can identify several characteristics of Groupthink. We see a fear of judgment along with someone going along with the ideas of a group because they do not want to disrupt harmony. Honestly, the boss probably offered Julie this opportunity to see what she would do when confronted with adversity. Intimidation is also a factor. Even though Julie doesn't necessarily have any big ideas, her saying that the advertising techniques seem pretty run-of-the-mill may spark an idea in someone else's mind – it is the beauty of working in a team. Speak up! Nothing will happen if you don't try, but there is a fifty percent chance things could go right if you do try. This example identifies the dangers of Groupthink along with the benefits of using your voice.

Example 2:

Kelly is trying to decide where to go to college. She has visited twelve schools and eliminated eight simply because she did not like the atmosphere or their program. Using a spreadsheet, she has created a list of pros and cons for each school. She has included her must-haves on the spreadsheet and can narrow it down to one school. Because of this, she can commit to her school and focus on things like finding a roommate and applying for scholarships along with enjoying her final year of high school.

This example doesn't utilize Groupthink; however, we do see a good line of critical thought process. Deciding which college to attend is a big life decision, and it should be considered thoroughly. Perhaps it seems like a straightforward question. However, many factors should be considered. Kelly uses critical thinking instead of making a quick decision (we see her eliminate the action bias), and this allows her to be stress-free. Her thought process is logical, and she uses reason to answer her question. The "evidence" would be the different things that each school offered on her list of pros and cons. It is also important to note that the negatives played a role in her decision – in other words, the things that were absent from the school. This is the opposite of being one-sided because she did not just look at what she liked about a school. Each school was given a fair chance, and this allowed her to make the right decision for herself.

Chapter 3: 25 Cognitive Biases

We touched briefly on a few biases that would directly affect critical thinking. This chapter will be entirely dedicated to biases and how to combat them. Sometimes the best way to fight or eliminate something is to understand that it exists. The cognitive biases sometimes fly under our radar which is why they can cause so many problems. These cognitive biases are also known as Charlie Munger's cognitive biases and are well-known throughout the world. They are known in the psychological world as the "human misjudgments".

The following will provide you with a summary of each bias, a few examples throughout, and a few tools to help you overcome cognitive bias in your own life. This will allow you to think critically and more efficiently.

Lollapalooza Tendencies

This type of bias generally comes about when people are in a group. This is because it is natural for humans to imitate those around them, in other words, fitting in. Lollapalooza states that the inherent tendencies and biases ingrained in the human system have the ability to sway our decision-making. When multiple biases are in action at the same time, the Lollapalooza effect is created. This is easier to understand when you put it in a real-life setting.

Charlie Munger referred to bidding wars at an auction as a creation of the Lollapalooza Effect. How? Well, when a group of people begins bidding each other up on an item that they may not even want that badly, we see a few biases come together and act at once which can cause poor decision-making.

Twaddle Tendency

This occurs when you spend too much time doing unimportant things. Wasting time on your cell phone is a big one in recent times. The twaddle tendency also occurs when you spend time talking about nothing – small talk – or when you fill your research papers with useless fluff just to add to the page count. To think critically, the faster you can get to the root of the problem, the sooner you will be able to solve it.

Inconsistency-Avoidance Tendency

Sometimes change is scary, as this leads to someone favoring familiarity over the unknown. The brain also naturally favors familiarity because it tries to conserve as much programming space as possible. This functions as a form of Darwinism and allowed people to make decisions quickly when they were traveling in groups during hunter-gatherer times. However, as frightening as it can be, change is good. Embrace it, especially when you are trying to eliminate the inconsistency avoidance bias in your everyday life. We don't need to travel in groups anymore, and our thought processing is much more complex. Treat it that way by expressing opinions and exploring as many options as possible.

Liking/Loving Tendency

This has a large presence in the lives of celebrities and the way that we treat our family members. To you, this may be known as favoritism. To Charles Munger, this was the liking/loving tendency. Have you ever defended a sibling in an argument even if she was in the wrong because you feel that blood is thicker than water? If so, you have succumbed to your brain's natural tendency to favor those you have feelings of love and admiration for. Loyalty can be a bad trait when trying to think critically. This is intermixed with emotion, and we've stated before that you should remove emotion from a situation as much as possible in order to think clearly. This stands true when combating the liking/loving tendency.

Doubt-Avoidance Tendency

Let's say your mom always told you that bananas were bad for you as a child. However, when you begin to get frequent muscle cramps, your doctor says bananas are a good source of potassium and will reduce cramping. The doubt-avoidance tendency would prompt you to disregard and even totally ignore this information because it goes against what you think you have always known. By ignoring this information, what you've always believed has to be right because there is no evidence against it.

Reward Punishment Bias

This is important to understand. People will respond better to an offering of an incentive than to the threat of punishment. By looking forward to a reward, people will perform more enthusiastically, and this increases the quality of work. Threatening to punish people can do two different things. First, they can become timider, and their work will not be great because they fear to make a mistake or they will become full of disdain since they feel threatened. This will also lessen the quality of work. So this may not be a bias you can avoid; however, it is something you should be aware of when you are assigning projects at work or maybe creating a practice schedule for a sports team. Both of these will require critical thinking and predictions about how people are going to react to a certain situation.

Hating/Disliking Bias

Are you good at holding grudges? If you answered yes, then you probably frequently succumb to the hating/disliking bias. Similar to the loving/liking bias, the hating/disliking bias will lead you to disregard the thoughts of people you don't favor. If you don't like the source of information, you are likely to ignore this information even if it supports your viewpoint. Holding a grudge will increase this tendency. So, let it go. Don't waste your energy on past fights. Let the past be the past and understand how someone being on your side is beneficial, especially if this person has the ability to shed light on a situation or answer some important questions.

Kantian Fairness Tendency

Life is not always going to be fair. The sooner you accept this, the better off you will be. However, the Kantian Fairness Tendency deals directly with man's inability to accept that the world works in mysterious ways and is unfair sometimes. It also states that a little unfairness toward an individual should be understood so long as it benefits the group or results in fairness for the majority in the long run. This also goes against the individualism that many Americans believe in. Seeing as we are not hunter-gatherers anymore, we can focus more on ourselves. This is why we have such a hard time accepting unfairness toward an individual.

Now, when referring to an individual's sacrifice to benefit the group, you may go toward the big picture thinking. For example, the way a soldier at war is treated may not be fair. However, in the long run, his efforts will benefit or even save, the lives of others. Or you can look at this from a much less imperative standpoint. Offering someone your store card at the grocery store so they can get the discounts would fit because you hope that they would do the same for you if your position were flipped.

Envy/Jealousy Tendency

Charles Munger's definition and example of this primal isn't as apparent in first-world countries as in other places. The envy/jealousy tendency is as simple as wanting what someone else has. Think of when you were a child in a room full of toys, but the only toy you were interested in playing with was the one your brother was playing with. Funny how that works, right? That would be the envy/jealousy tendency in action. Like many of the biases, the first step to combatting bias is to recognize its involvement in your life.

Influence From Mere Association Tendency

This bias is the reason we see celebrities in advertisements. Celebrities have a large impact on the lives of many, and if you see Rihanna in a shirt, chances are, if you are a fan, you will want that shirt too. Even if Rihanna did not take part in the creation of the shirt, she still has a part in selling the shirt because people want to be like her. A lot of times, we take cues from the people we admire. This is the same reason why so many different dieting programs take off, even if they are not that great.

Excessive Self-Regard Tendency

As humans, we all have a tendency to believe we are above average. This bias is the root of overconfidence, and if you are familiar with Rhonda Rousey's loss to Holly Holmes in a UFC match a few years ago, you see where overconfidence can be dangerous. Being aware of this bias is important because it can keep your ego in check. Being egotistical can cause your judgment to be clouded which makes thinking critically more difficult than it has to be. This will also lead you to make poor decisions because you believe you have the ability to do more than you actually can.

Let's say that in college you played a bit of division one baseball. Twenty years later, your ten-year-old son and his friends are over and want to play a bit of backyard baseball, so you decide to join in. You are thinking about how good at baseball you were back then and decide things can't have changed that much, except that you now work in an office from nine to five on weekdays and have yet to get that gym membership you have been talking about. The next day, you can't understand why you can barely move, and your ankles are swollen. This would be the excessive self-regard tendency at work.

Over-optimism Tendency

Though many people like things from an idealistic standpoint, real life does not always work out the way that we expect it to. This is where being overly optimistic can get you in trouble. It can also lead you to believe that a bad thing that happened to someone else will never happen to you. For example, many of us take texting and driving far too lightly despite the large number of people that die in car accidents caused by cell phone usage each year. This is because even though we hear about these accidents, we will not believe they can happen to us until they do. Therefore, we refuse to take the correct precautions which include putting away our phones.

Deprival Super Reaction Tendency

It has been said that humans react more to losses than to gains and would rather have no gain than any type of loss. This comes to the forefront of our minds when we are facing impending loss. This is why gambling can be an issue. When you lose money while gambling, you are tempted to continue gambling just so that you can make back what you lost. Loss can create anxiety and stress which can overtake a person's mind and consume their thoughts.

Curiosity Tendency

People are naturally curious; however, it is those who push their curiosity to the next level who are most successful. This is a human trait that many people do not exploit. According to Munger, you should push your boundaries and find out everything you can about everything. The more that you know, the better off you will be. Even though this has never been mentioned specifically in this piece until now, it is obvious how important the curiosity tendency is when thinking critically. We have talked about how you should know everything you can about a situation to make accurate evaluations. If you do not regularly exploit the curiosity tendency, you will find yourself unable to reach the highest level of critical thinking.

Reciprocation Tendency

Believe it or not, humans don't like to be indebted to each other. The reciprocation tendency requires that when someone does us a favor, we feel compelled to do a favor for them. This can be beneficial and detrimental because sometimes the urge to return a favor can lead us to make a poor decision.

Munger added to this by saying that when you ask for something, start high. For example, if you need fifty dollars from your mother to buy a ticket to an amusement park, ask for seventy dollars initially. This way, if she refuses, your second offer will be what you actually need. She will be more likely to give you fifty dollars when you ask for more at the start than giving you fifty dollars outright.

Simple, Pain-Avoiding Psychological Denial

Ignorance is bliss, "they say". Except when you are attempting to think critically. Then ignorance is not so great. However, when dealing with painful situations, humans have a tendency to deny and ignore the facts instead of facing them to protect themselves, especially when what they have been told does not affect their daily living. This can occur when a mother is told her son will not be returning from war because he died during combat. The news is easy to deny because she has no concrete evidence. In her mind, he is still overseas fighting, but alive. Until she has a body in a coffin, she will be unable to come to terms with the fact that her son will never be returning home.

Drug Misinfluence Tendency

Rather than an unconscious tendency, this one can be influenced by outside forces. It is generally a supplement that helps a person cope with simple, pain-avoiding psychological denial in order to make reality more bearable. For example, after the funeral, the mother can no longer deny that her son is dead. So she turns to drugs like pain pills to ease her suffering, and this becomes her way of coping. This is unhealthy and can have tragic consequences. People who self-harm would also fall under this category. Even though they are not taking any physical drugs, the actions of harming themselves create a feeling of euphoria and a sense of doing the right thing because they believe they should be harmed. The drug misinfluence tendency can be difficult to identify because of the previous bias. These two are unique because of how intertwined they are.

Use-It Or Lose-It Tendency

The brain is like a sponge in the way it retains information. When you continuously use a sponge, it will stay wet, porous, and continue absorbing. Then when you put the sponge down, the water it has absorbed slowly leaks out until the sponge becomes dry and shriveled from disuse. This is kind of what the definition of the use-it or lose-it tendency tries to capture. When a person is continuously learning and applying this knowledge to their life, the brain will continue to accept it. However, if you stop learning, or decrease the amount of information you take in on a regular basis, your brain will adjust to that. As a result, you could suffer from a diminishing brain capacity and an inability to retain and use the information you learn. When you continuously practice a skill, the brain is less likely to lose it, and it will be easier to recall the next time you do it.

Availability Misweighing Tendency

When evaluating a situation, the brain automatically will use what is available to it and forget anything else due to limited brain capacity. This is why you are more likely to complete a task if you write it down first or work from a list, such as when you're at the grocery store and forget the list at home. You are likely to get the first and last thing that you wrote on the list but will forget what you were supposed to get if it was written in the middle of the list. Also, have you ever said "I'll know it when I see it" or "I'll remember her name when she tells me again"? This is because of the availability misweighing tendency where the saying "out of sight, out of mind" reigns true. You should be careful when problem-solving if this tendency is apparent. A lot of times, the things you remember the most clearly will be considered more thoroughly than something that is less memorable. However, even the facts that seem unimportant can be important.

Stress-Influence Tendency

In some cases, light stress can actually improve performance. However, extreme stress will cause a rush of adrenaline and the urge to make a hard and fast decision. Long periods of stress can cause pessimistic feelings to take over and can cause overbearing fatigue. Both of these can stop productivity altogether. We must understand that stress can cause a number of different reactions. This should be considered when problem-solving. You must also acknowledge that everyone is going to react differently to stress as we are all unique individuals.

Reason Respecting Tendency

People are more prone to learning when why they are learning makes sense. Appealing to reason is important in many aspects of life. When attempting to teach someone, you should make sure they know why they are learning about a topic to get them to engage in the activity. Do not just give out orders when leading someone. This tendency does have some drawbacks. People are prone to learning even if the reasoning is meaningless or incorrect. This can be seen when teaching a child that they must wash behind their ears otherwise potatoes will grow there. Obviously, you should wash behind your ears, but potatoes are never going to grow behind your ears no matter how long you neglect them. Hopefully, an adult would not believe this, but this example was simple.

Authority Misinfluence Tendency

Throughout all of history, we see leaders and followers. We also see how much a leader's decisions can affect the lives of those following them. There can be serious consequences if the leader is wrong – war, for example, can lead to the death of many with little benefit and is the decision of the leader. You can also misinterpret the leader's commands which causes you to do the wrong thing. A good example refers to a nurse who incorrectly reads a doctor's shorthand and administers treatment to the wrong area on a patient. Following instructions can be difficult because if the instructions are strange, and you do not have anyone to ask about them, they can be misinterpreted.

Senescence Misinfluence Tendency

As you age, your cognitive abilities decay. This is where the saying "can't teach an old dog new tricks" comes from because it is more difficult for old people to retain information due to decreasing brain capacity. Sometimes this can be difficult to recognize because they make an effort to 'keep up with the times' from a social aspect. For example, my grandmother purchased many Apple products later in life and spent a lot of time playing the same games that I did. However, she took a lot of time to write text messages and never really got the hang of taking photos from these devices. From the surface, her cognitive decay was not very obvious, but once you got a closer look, there were signs.

Contrast Misreaction Tendency

When evaluating two things side by side, we begin to look at the similarities and differences between the two instead of looking at the things as separate entities. This can cause problems because when trying to decide between the two different things, you may decide you like the pros of one better than the cons of the other instead of actually liking your choice. We can take it back to making a college decision. When making this choice, you may be looking at two different schools that do not really have all that you want, but one shines brighter than the other, so you choose that one. However, if you had looked at each separately, your dislike of them both may have led you to a different school that was a better fit for you.

This affects decision-making in a number of ways. For example, when purchasing a new car, you may select a few upgrades because the amount for the upgrades seems small in comparison to the price of the car. However, both are unnecessary and probably expensive. Also, when marrying again, your new spouse may seem a lot better than your previous one. However, this could be because of the bad memories that surround your ex-spouse. This occurs when comparing two things instead of appraising something on its own.

Social Proof Tendency

This is the automatic tendency of man to think and do as others around him. For example, when you are new at school and on your way to lunch, instead of figuring out where the cafeteria is for yourself, it is easier to follow someone else who is going to the cafeteria. This goes along with the idea that you will imitate the actions of those around you. This is why your parents may not like the group of friends you are hanging out with. Though you like them and are a good kid, your friends may not be the best which can influence the decisions that you make. However, if you hang out with the future valedictorian, you will be more likely to study hard and score better on exams. It is important for societies to stop the spread of bad behavior and show an appreciation for good behavior because of the social proof tendency.

This bias is occurring when Groupthink is in action. Although we are all unique individuals, we have a tendency to imitate those around us. We can even think in ways similar to those around us. This reduces creativity and limits our problem-solving abilities. When in a group, you should focus on combatting this by using the same strategies you would use to combat Groupthink.

Remember, these tendencies will be reflected in your own thoughts when trying to unravel and solve a problem and are important for you to recognize. However, they will also become apparent in the actions of anyone else who is involved in your situation. Learning all of these biases is important because you must be able to recognize them. If you don't have them all down before you begin your problem-solving journey, and you are unsure of whether or not someone is showing a tendency, look it up! Whether you use this book or an online search, the 25 cognitive biases can be found in many different places.

Combatting these tendencies can be easily recognized when they are present, and you are taking note of them. These biases are not permanent, and steps can be taken to lessen their appearance in your thoughts. Being self-aware and understanding where the bias comes from are two steps that you have probably already taken while reading this. However, there is a test called the Implicit Association Test that can be utilized if you're still having a difficult time being self-aware. Talking with others about your beliefs, especially those who oppose your beliefs, can be beneficial because you are not only learning about others but also how to become more empathetic. You can also write about your encounters with others and try to track where biases make appearances in your life. As you go along, you can try to minimalize these appearances.

In the following, we will identify and discuss a few cognitive biases at work.

Win An Argument Every Time

By utilizing critical thinking and understanding the 25 cognitive biases, you will be able to form an argument. However, there is more involved in arguing. There is also more that can affect your argument, aside from the 25 cognitive biases. To do this, you must first understand what an argument is made of in order to form an argument of your own.

When you are making an argument, you can utilize the skills you learned in the chapter about thinking like a lawyer.

If you look way back to ancient times, the logic of Aristotle remains true even though thousands of years have passed. His argument consisted of two main parts: the premise and the conclusion. A premise is going to support the claim that is being made. Think of this as the supporting details. The conclusion is going to be the claim that is being made. However, to get to the conclusion, your premise must be logical and lead to the conclusion. When creating an effective argument, you want your reasoning to be sound – don't leave anything out. Make sure that the premise or premises support the argument. When all of your premise/s support the argument, the argument becomes valid. You also cannot twist the truth in any of your premises if you are looking to create a sound argument.

Let's look at a valid argument and an invalid argument. Each of these will have two premises and one conclusion. An argument can have several premises and a single conclusion and still be valid. In fact, the more supportive premises you have, the more sound your argument will become.

All men are mortal. This is a premise. It is a fact rather than an opinion.

Socrates is a man. This is another premise. It is also a fact, and the conclusion will help link the two premises to each other.

This means Socrates is mortal.

The next example is an invalid argument.

Socrates is mortal. True, this is the conclusion that we came to in the previous argument. What goes wrong is in the next premise.

All men are mortal. This is also true. It is the conclusion that is illogical.

This means Socrates is a man. This is a true statement. However, just because Socrates is mortal does not mean he is a man. All animals are also mortal. Based on the information that the premises provide, you cannot automatically assume that Socrates is a man.

There are also inductive arguments. However, when trying to apply critical thinking to an argument while thinking like a lawyer, these are not the best because they are based on assumptions.

The following is an inductive argument about the diets of Greeks.

Most Greeks eat fish.

Socrates is Greek.

Socrates eats fish.

This argument is inductive because you are using reasoning to figure out what kind of food Socrates would have eaten. Inductive means inferring general laws based on particular instances. We can assume that since Greeks rely heavily on fish for nutrients, Socrates would eat fish. When making an inductive argument, there are weak and strong arguments, and they are not going to be absolute. There will always be an outlier.

So, we have seen a good argument and a bad argument. Now we can talk about what not to include in your argument along with what an argument is *not*.

1. Assertions: A confident, forceful statement of fact or belief. The key part of this definition is belief. This allows for opinions to be involved. While there are different types of arguments, you should understand that in this case, we need to argue facts. For example, saying that Muslims are bad is not an argument. It is a statement that would need to be supported by facts, or in our case, premises. It is also a belief.
2. Statements: Einstein said, "God does not play dice with the universe." Is Einstein an intelligent human? Yes. Does this mean we should listen to everything he says and use it in a literal sense? No.
3. Explanations: Because Caesar's army was outnumbered, they retreated across the Rhine. This is true, but it is not arguing anything. In fact, there is nothing here to argue.
4. Opinions: Cannot stress this enough! Leave your opinions and emotions out of the picture!

A good argument will not include statements, and it will not attack the person making the opposing argument. This is called *ad hominem*. To combat *ad hominem*, you should refrain from involving emotions and disallow them from swaying your argument. *Ad hominem* can also be applied to assigning guilt due to association.

Let's expand upon the cognitive biases and talk about a few other things that can affect your argument and how it stands up against the arguments of others. For example, saying that one restaurant is better than another because your favorite celebrity is on the commercials does not make it a sound or valid argument. The celebrity does not determine the taste of the food or the speed of the service at the restaurant.

Appealing to pity is a good persuasive technique, but to create an argument that will stand on its own, you need factual information. So avoid the appeal to pity as one of your main points. When you are appealing to pity, often a visual aid is required to create the impact you are looking for.

When creating an argument, first you should rely on cold, hard facts. This is where statistics come in handy. Using statistics can create the same effect that visuals can, but there is only one way to interpret them. We often see the appeal to pity in propaganda. The same can be said about an appeal to fear. Any threats that include a threat to someone's life or someone's freedom should not be considered a main point. These can be utilized as supporting details, but ending your argument with threats will not result in a valid argument. If you are arguing that something must be good since there is no evidence to oppose or validate the argument, and thus an argument cannot be made, then don't try to make one. For example, let's say that you decided to argue that cotton must be good for you since there is no research stating otherwise you would not be correct. This is known as the appeal to ignorance.

Other things to consider when creating an argument include sweeping generalizations and selective observation. Sweeping generalizations occur when you take one instance and apply it to all situations. For example, you should never lie. However, if someone arrived at your house with a gun and asked if you had any children, what would you say? Lying and saying no could protect the lives of your children. In this case, telling the truth could put them in danger.

Selective observation is the act of only seeing information that will support your argument. When you use this in your argument, you allow the opposer to find the holes in your argument very easily which makes for a weak argument. Wishful thinking can also affect your argument. Remember, just because you wish for something to be true, does not mean it is. For example, let's say that you put your plastic and paper product in separate containers so that the trash disposal will recycle them. You say you are helping the environment, but really the company puts your recyclables in with the rest of the garbage. You are only seeing the part of the process that is supporting your belief that you are helping the environment.

In addition, just because the argument you want to make is not the most popular argument, it can still be sound, and by making your argument strong, people may actually learn that it is the better argument. For example, school uniforms are somewhat controversial. However, in recent times, many schools have switched over to uniforms due to the practicality. Do not allow the opinions of others sway your own. You should make observations, do research, and draw conclusions on your own. By doing this, you will be able to make your argument more convincing because while it is factual, you also believe it.

The example of an invalid argument uses circular reasoning because only one of the premises assumes the conclusions. All evidence must be included in your argument to come to the most logical conclusion. You should also focus on keeping your argument consistent. When researching, you should find multiple dependable sources that share consistent information. The more support your argument has, the stronger it will be.

In addition, remember that two wrongs do not make a right. For example, Allan's mother shot her husband because he beat her every night. Allan's mother is not justified because there are other ways to solve her problem. Quoting out of context is also not okay when trying to make a strong argument. Sure, you don't have to quote entire books word for word, but you should consider all of the information a source provides instead of just the information that supports your stance. You should consider this when using quotes.

Do not cut off a quote before the "but" comes. If there is a "but" and you ignore it, your argument will be weakened.

Writing Critically and Writing a Clear Argument

Writing critically is very important in academic writing. In your English classes, you will be asked to write at least one argumentative paper that will ask you to defend one side or another. Critical writing can be broken down. To put it simply, critical writing evaluates and analyzes more than one source in order to develop an argument. This is different than descriptive writing which describes what something is like. However, description will be involved in your critical writing along with explanation. There should be a good balance between analysis and description. Critical thinking will make your writing clearer and more concise. This allows you to make well-thought-out arguments in a shorter amount of time with more success. Being clear will increase readability. This will allow for a wider audience and a more enjoyable read. When writing, sometimes it is difficult to put your thoughts on paper without sounding crazy. Being told to write more clearly is a lot easier than actually writing clearly. Therefore, this is going to give you a few tips and pointers on becoming a better writer.

At this point, you have heard a lot about how to think critically, cognitive biases, and how to escape the trap Groupthink creates. Now, you will be able to write critically. When you are writing critically, you'll be able to word your thoughts better, and your paragraphs will be more useful – it won't just be about word counts anymore, but the word counts will be met regardless.

The following is a series of questions you can ask. These can be applied to writing and editing your writing:

Is your idea/argument a good or bad one?

Is my argument valid and defensible? Is it the opposite?

We have talked about how to determine whether an argument is valid, but you also need to be able to defend your argument with premises and supporting details. If you cannot do this, your point of view will be easy to poke holes in and will collapse like a house of cards.

Is my position on the issue rational and reasonable?

Reason is something we have already talked about quite a bit. It is important because it will justify your position.

Do I deal with the complexity of the situation or do I only utilize clichés and stereotypes to make my point?

Stereotypes are not foolproof; therefore, they should not be used in an argument because there are many instances where they will not be true. The same goes for clichés. Clichés are overused and only occur in a perfect situation.

Do I touch deeper points, or do I only scrape the surface when talking about my topic?

Go into detail! Details are so important, and the more valid support you have for your argument, the better. Don't be repetitive, but present as many different details as you can, especially in the first draft of your writing. You should strive to understand what you are writing about and encourage your readers to understand what they are reading.

Do I address the other points of view properly?

Always consider the counterarguments. These are going to test your own viewpoint, and those who support the counterarguments are going to be looking for things that will take your argument down.

Do I question my own ideas and test them for validity?

Question all of the evidence you find and make sure it is supported by things like experiments and observation. If there are surveys involved in your argument, make sure the pool of people surveyed is an accurate proportion.

Do I have specific goals in mind with this piece?

Create a goal and write it down. This will help you stick with the purpose of your argument.

When forming an argument and writing about it, you are going to need to give yourself time and be very organized. Your first step should be to research. Utilize all outlets that you have access to. Go to the library and read as much as you can about your topic first and write down important points and supporting details. Then, if you have access to any online databases, use those. Generally, depending on your topic, you will find statistics and experiments. Do not disregard anything because it does not directly address your viewpoint. Anything you can learn is good. The more you broaden your knowledge on the topic, the easier it will be for you to argue one way or another. You never know – halfway through, you may discover that you actually think the opposing viewpoint is better. Once you have searched databases, go to the search engines, and you will find the opinions of others and some more supporting details. The more information that you have and know about a topic, the easier your thoughts will flow. At this point, you should have several more sources than what is required. By the end, you will have to cut down the number of sources because you should not need them all.

Next, you should make outlines. That's right, multiple. Each should get more detailed, and by the end, you will have a sentence outline. This is essentially your first draft with different numbers and sections. You may think that making multiple outlines is excessive, but it will allow you to see your information in several different ways. When you look at information in the same font in block paragraphs, it is difficult to determine whether or not it will be clear to readers. This is why having someone else edit it is important. Furthermore, if you don't have someone else, as long as you have given yourself enough time, you can put the project away and look at it the next day.

Your writing should not be confusing or full of hidden meaning. Make it as clear as possible. When you go through and edit, you should determine whether the following questions are easily found:

Is the purpose of the piece clear and easily found?
Stating the purpose in the first paragraph is the easiest way to do this. You are not trying to conceal your topic. There is no harm in including it in the some of your first thoughts.

What questions does this piece answer? What questions are explored?

From what perspective is my argument?
You should know this for a couple of different reasons. Understanding your own perspective will allow you to write about it clearer. It will also allow you to determine the opposing viewpoints and determine counterarguments.

Where did I get my information? Are the sources valid? Was the information consistent in all of my sources?

What concepts are central in my line of thinking?
These would be your main points, a common number of main points is three, but you can have any number of main points to support your argument. These main points will have supporting details. They can be considered the premises of your arguments. When we talked about things like quotes in the cognitive biases chapter, they were not to be used in an argument. Using them as supporting details is acceptable as long as you can explain why they are supportive to your argument.

What conclusions am I making? What premises do I include?
These, of course, would be your entire argument. If you use a thesis statement, which you should, your premises and your conclusions will be found here. Your thesis statement will only feature your premises and your conclusion. Write the premises in the order that they will appear to make the thesis statement more usable.

Am I making any assumption/s? Are these assumptions that I should be making?

There is a difference between making an educated inference and just making assumptions. For example, if there are no clouds in the sky, we can assume it is not going to rain. However, just because George Clooney is not your father does not mean you can assume he is your best friend's father. You must have evidence to support this.

As a writer who writes critically, you should be able to evaluate your work thoroughly. The questions above will help you with this. While you write, you will use several different levels of thinking: validity, context, accuracy, and precision. The conclusions you make should be predictable when paired with all of the evidence you gathered. Always keep your argument reasonable, solid, and valid. In addition, you should always consider any weaknesses your argument has along with potential counterarguments. How does considering counterarguments help you? Well, you will be able to strengthen your own argument by pointing out the weaknesses in the counterarguments. You can also block the holes in your own argument by strategizing and using critical thinking. Make your weaknesses seem like strengths in an argument.

Writing is important and can help you think critically successfully. Writing requires you to do two things: write out your thoughts completely and make them readable to a varied audience. Thinking critically is like speaking proper English to someone who learned it as a second language. You may be introducing a concept completely new to your audience. This requires you to be extremely thorough, and you must know your topic completely. Your awareness of a topic will increase when you write it out, and complex problems can be worked through and solved.

Here are five steps that will aid you in the process of gathering evidence:

1. Question everything and actively try to find new information. Examine, parse, and validate every piece of information you plan to utilize in your argument.

2. Don't jump to conclusions or make assumptions. Come to a conclusion based on the evidence you have and not the evidence you don't have. In addition, you should determine whether or not your argument is too general. Are there other explanations?

3. Keep your writing from repeating itself. When making an argument, redundancy can take over and weaken your argument. This is why it is so important to find as much information as you can. In addition, avoid truisms or self-evident truths.

4. Do not oversimplify things. Use detailed explanations that go into depth.

5. Find the holes in all arguments, including your own.

How do you determine if your writing is poor?

• The thesis is repetitive and does not indicate where the rest of the writing will lead. You are trying to write an informative, argumentative piece, not a mystery. Keep it clear all the way through.

• If you rely on simple summaries instead of explanations that have a lot of details, it is likely that there is not enough evidence to support your argument. This makes for a weak argument that is vague and lacks readability because things are not thoroughly explained. When talking about relationships between concepts, explain why they exist instead of stating that they exist.

• If your argument is disorganized, the reader will be able to tell. Disorganization is bad. It muddies the purpose and makes the argument unclear. Make sure everything is well-ordered. If you are explaining a step-by-step process, you need to make sure the steps are in order. If you utilize historical references, make sure that they are ordered chronologically.

• If you present ideas but not their relation to the argument, you are doing it wrong. Explanations are important! People are reading this so that they can understand your point of view!

• If your conclusions are not supported by your premises, your writing is not only bad, but your argument is also invalid. If your premises are incorrect, your conclusions are invalid.

• You use several sources and attempt to string their ideas together without actually analyzing what is being said. You must analyze what is being said instead of accepting it to be true.

Another important part of critical writing is the revision process. Revisions will not only refine your writing but are also intended to make your piece clearer. To make your argument better, play the devil's advocate. Present the article to yourself and decide what you would say to combat your own argument. Then, fill in the holes in your own argument. Repeat the revision process as many times as you can.

You can also look at your argument in different forms. This will help you see different strengths and weakness along with more ways to expand your argument. Review the evidence you found, depending on the argument. New evidence will likely come up. Using new evidence will strengthen your argument if it supports it. If a new argument that counters yours is discovered, you need to be able to combat this evidence and figure out how it will affect your point of view. The revision process will help you add to your argument, sure, but it will also help you remove the clutter or arguments that are no longer valid. If this argument is being made over a long period of time, you must constantly be revising your article. Pay attention to the start and end dates of your project to make sure you are as accurate as possible.

Find someone who has the opposing argument. Sometimes, in school, your instructor will assign someone to an opposing viewpoint. If possible, collaborate and use each other to strengthen your argument. This will also save you both some time because you can do your own research and come together. Hearing a voice other than your own can help you in several different ways. They can push your arguments to the limit which will require you to re-evaluate your argument. You can also see if your words make sense coming from someone else or if your point of view has any cognitive biases present.

Lastly, in a best-case scenario, the critical thinker you shared your piece with reaches the same conclusions you did base on the premises you provided, and your argument is solid. During this process, always be as aware as possible and stay open-minded. Being faithful to your position in an argument is important and so is being open to other possibilities.

Chapter 4: Convergent and Divergent Thinking

Convergent Thinking

When you break down the term convergent thinking, you come out with two pieces: convergent can mean a variety of ideas coming together to form one specific conclusion. Thinking is obviously what we have been talking about throughout this entire book.

When you put the terms together, convergent thinking can be defined as a problem-solving technique that enables a variety of different people from different backgrounds and occupations to come to the best conclusion about a clear, well-understood question. This thinking strategy is used to develop a fast, logical answer to a problem. By using convergent thinking, a group can solve problems at a faster pace as long as they can agree on an answer. This train of thought can be considered lacking in creativity, but it is efficient. Therefore, while it has cons, it also has pros. This type of thinking is good for obtaining straightforward facts, such as the sky is blue and the Earth is round.

Convergent thinking is used in any standard IQ test. It is also used when there is only one correct answer to a problem. We can say that math problems will utilize a lot of convergent thinking. These tests evaluate things such as pattern recognition, logical flow of thought, and your capacity to solve problems. Multiple choice questions are also a way to test convergent thinking.

Divergent Thinking

Divergent thinking is defined as a problem-solving strategy which allows a person to see multiple correct answers to a problem and determine which one will work the best. This type of thought process involves creativity and allows you to look at multiple things at once. You use divergent thinking when you are brainstorming ideas for a paper or freewriting. Through divergence, a person is able to take one idea or statement and branch off to make several different conclusions about that statement. All of these conclusions can be considered correct, and the conclusions will vary depending on the person.

There are 8 elements of divergent thinking:

1. *Complexity*: This is your ability to theorize many different ideas that are multilayered.
2. *Risk-taking*: This is important when considering your ability to set yourself apart from others. Those who venture into the unknown are generally the ones who make new discoveries and find new answers to questions.
3. *Elaboration*: This is taking one idea and building off of it.
For example, Hershey's Chocolate has grown from a simple chocolate bar to several different types of chocolate in different forms which allows for a greater amount of productivity.
4. *Originality*: This is why it is so incredible to see several different people use divergent thinking to come up with an answer to a problem. People will utilize many different trains of thought to come up with new ideas.
5. *Imagination*: This is important in creating new products and developing new ideas. This also will connect to originality.

6. *Flexibility*: Your ability to create varied perceptions and categories. This is how we get several variations of the same thing.

7. *Curiosity*: To create new ideas, you must come up with new questions and inquiries.

8. *Fluency*: The ability to stimulate many ideas to have many different solutions in case one works better than the other.

People who think divergently share traits such as an inability to conform, persistence, curiosity, and readiness to take risks. There are no personality traits associated with those who engage in convergent thinking. This means that all people engage in convergent thinking. There are no tests to determine divergent thinking.

The two different thinking styles can be compared in several different ways. Studies show that divergent thinking and convergent thinking can affect mood. When prompted to use divergent thinking, a positive mood was triggered, increasing productivity. When prompted to use convergent thinking, a negative mood was triggered. Divergent thinkers generally score higher in categories that test word fluency and reading ability.

Divergent thinking is necessary for open-ended problems with even the smallest bit of creativity. Things like sleep deprivation can decrease your ability to think divergently. However, sleep deprivation hardly affects convergent thinking.

Let's look at some examples.

An example of a question that would require convergent thinking would look like this:

Who was the first president of the United States?

a. George Washington
b. Barack Obama
c. Thomas Jefferson
d. Abraham Lincoln

There is only one true answer to this problem – George Washington. This type of problem would not require any critical thinking and is simply asking for a recitation of your memory.

An example of a question that would require divergent thinking would look like this:

Who was the most influential president of the United States?

There is not one right answer to this question. As long as you were able to gather sufficient evidence, you could choose any president that you wanted. This question requires creativity and would call for originality, as long as you weren't copying off of the person next to you. If you chose a president who maybe did not have a great impact, you would be taking a risk that could benefit you in the long run as long as you played your cards right.

So how does this all play into critical thinking?

I said before that convergent thinking does not require any critical thought. This remains true. You would utilize convergent thinking when acquiring information. A good example of a convergent thinker is Sherlock Holmes. He used deductive reasoning to solve a slew of crimes. He was able to take in all of the details of a crime scene and make connections to come to one conclusion and answer the question of who committed the crime. This sums up the description and analysis portion of our critical thinking model.

Once you delve into the evaluation portion of our model, you are making the transition to divergent thinking. Divergent thinking would take the answer of who committed the crime and ask more questions about it. For example, once you figure out who committed the crime, you will want to know why the crime was committed, what crimes could be committed in the future, etc. Through divergent thinking, we can create profiles and answer questions about future crimes which lead to more efficient problem-solving. This is where you will begin to see that critical thinking is more of a cycle than a step-by-step process. You can pick up at any point in the critical thinking process and continue onward around and around.

Chapter 5: What Lawyers Can Teach You About Learning How to Think

Part 1: Spotting Issues

Approach the issue from all angles. We have talked several times about considering all points of view. Lawyers must do this every day in order to build a strong case. This will allow you to be more empathetic, and it will improve your critical thinking. The more you practice finding the different angles, the easier it will become.

Avoid emotional entanglement. You have heard this before too! Leaving emotions out of it will allow you to think clearly. Focusing on the facts will decrease the fluff in your answers, creating clear, concise solutions. This will also save time and resources.

Argue both sides. Not only does this help you understand the weaknesses of the other argument, but it will also help you make yours shine brighter. The contrast-misinfluence tendency can be played in your favor. Making their side look bad will make your argument shine brighter. If you are expected to work as a team, understanding the other side's point of view will create a greater amount of tolerance.

Part 2: Using Logic

Use deductive reasoning. Use patterns of law to draw connections.

Example: a dirty dog shows negligence. Charlene's dog is not dirty, so she probably takes care of her dog. We do not know yet that Charlene's dog is well taken care of, but we can assume a healthy coat means a healthy dog.

Construct syllogisms. A syllogism states that what is true for a group will also be true for the individual members of said group. Syllogisms have three parts: a general statement, a particular statement, and a conclusion about the particular based on the general. For example, the high school's senior class trip was a day trip to Six Flags. Since we know this information, when we pass the bus, we can assume that all of the students on the bus are seniors.

Infer general rules from patterns of specifics. Inductive reasoning allows you to think that if something causes the same result a number of times, a rule can be formed. When Joey eats peanut butter, he starts to swell up and has trouble breathing. We can assume that Joey is allergic to peanut butter.

Compare similar situations using analogies. Lawyers sometimes argue a case by using comparisons to earlier cases. You can do this in your everyday life. Katie has seen her brother and his girlfriend hold hands and kiss. She has also seen her mother and father hold hands and kiss. With this information, Katie can compare the two and decide that the relationships are similar and use them as reference points.

Ask why. Laws are made with the reason why serving as its 'policy'. This can be used to argue that new facts should be used under the same law or that new laws should be created because the policy no longer covers all of the facts. Do not take anything for granted and make sure you have a thorough understanding of what laws mean along with why they were created if you truly want to think like a lawyer.

Accept ambiguity. As much as you would like to believe it, not all things are going to be black and white. It is impossible to account for every possible outcome when creating a law. Therefore, ambiguity allows for laws to be more flexible. When you assume things, it is harder to get to the truth because assumptions are not always true. Lawyers only use proven facts in their arguments. Nothing is true without proof.

Thinking like a lawyer also means that you should always use your best judgment. Even if an argument is logical, that does not mean it is good. Using judgment will allow you to remove bad points from your main argument. For example, in Pennsylvania, drivers are supposed to yield to pedestrians. However, this does not mean you should cross the road if a car is coming. Although the driver is supposed to stop, they may not. Therefore, you should wait for them to stop before crossing.

Thinking like a lawyer can benefit you in many professions other than being an attorney or a judge. Thinking like a lawyer can aid you if you are an entrepreneur or even a content marketer. Thinking analytically like this can help you with your critical thinking simply because it is from a different point of view. Getting many different viewpoints can help your overall understanding of a topic and its importance.

Lawyers have many good characteristics that they are required to develop in their line of work. For example, they pay acute attention to detail, and almost nothing is going to pass by them. They are also able to acquire a lot of knowledge because of their attention to detail. This allows them to be extremely organized.

If you are a college student, thinking like a lawyer could be a good thing for you to develop. This will help you when writing persuasive essays and presenting speeches.

There are two different kinds of questions: closed and open. Start by asking basic questions. Think of this as writing a description. When you are deciding what to cook for dinner without going to the store, this can be useful. I would pick the first meal that came to mind and then search for the ingredients.

For example, I am looking to make some sort of pasta dish for dinner.

Do I have pasta? Yes.

This is a closed answer type of question. It can be expanded on, but the question is answered completely with just yes. For this case, I am going to expand and say that I found rigatoni noodles and penne pasta in the pantry. Both of these are suitable for dinner.

Next, I will ask another closed answer question.

Do I have any jar sauce? No.

Now I have run into a roadblock and must change paths because I don't have a jar sauce. I must come up with something different for dinner or make a sauce from scratch. I decide to make a sauce from scratch.

Do I have any canned tomato sauce? No.

Now I will have to decide on something else to make for dinner. I decide to look in the freezer.

Do I have any ready-to-eat meals? No.

Now, as you continue on with this thought process, you could ask yourself what a meal is. This is venturing into open-ended questions, and we see some possible divergent thinking involved here.

Another important part of asking questions to untangle the truth is questioning all assumptions. If we questioned all of the assumptions we made every day, we would probably not get everything done. It is okay to assume that the floor will be solid when you wake up in the morning and that your car will be working if it was fine the night before. However, some assumptions can be dangerous and will surely lead to miscommunication.

In an article I read, there was an example pertaining to office drama. A woman was upset, and things escalated very quickly, but nobody knew exactly what caused the outburst. This is where our wheels begin to turn in a dangerous direction. Our assumptions can be so powerful that we begin to form opinions and create emotions around things when we are not even sure of their authenticity. This can affect your personal relationships and other things, bigger things, like business relationships. By sticking to our assumptions, we enable ourselves to hold grudges, which can create biases and cloud judgment which affects the critical thinking process. We allow assumptions to have such great control over us because they make us feel like what we are doing is right, and humans like to be right.

So, how do you combat these assumptions? If you are unsure, *ask*. You can be unsure and diplomatic at the same time, and you must not always worry about whom you will offend. For example, when you were at the shore, you and your brother got into an argument. On the way home, you fell asleep in the car, and when he dropped you off at home, he did not say much. It is easy to assume his silence means that he is still angry, especially if you feel like you guys did not resolve things at the beach. When he goes back to the beach the next weekend with your sister, you think you know he is mad at you because he did not invite you – even though you had a conference in San Diego that weekend. Do you see where being emotionally involved in this situation after making an assumption can be bad? This is a poor display of critical thinking as well. You are too involved and not asking the right questions. Next time you see your brother, you should apologize and ask if he is still angry. If he is, then you should attempt to work out your differences.

Making assumptions is not the same as finding a solution to a problem. Learning how to solve problems face-to-face can be hard and scary, but at the end of the day, solving problems right away will help you learn from each other, and you might even get more help. Solving problems like this can also help us see connections between events and each other.

Asking questions about existing evidence is another way to find connections between two unlike things. You may also find out more things about the evidence. For example, let's say there was a jewel heist and only one jewel was missing in a store full of precious gems. You should begin asking questions about the remaining jewels to find out more complex questions. For example, what types of jewels were left behind? Compare this answer to the stolen jewel. You will continue asking questions until you are led to the reason why the jewel was stolen. Then, you can expand to the surrounding areas and see if other jewels were stolen. It is likely that they were stolen by the same person. Then you can gather evidence from both locations and go on and on until you eventually are bound to recover the missing jewels and the thief. This is critical thinking at work. You are utilizing divergent thinking and convergent thinking. Throughout this process, if you are interviewing witnesses, the cognitive biases will come into play, and they should be considered throughout the interview process.

Another thing you should consider throughout the investigation is who gathered the evidence. If it was yourself, you should make a note of how you collected it. Did you follow protocol? What was out of the ordinary? Do not make assumptions. If you have a suspect in mind, add them to the list, but do not let thoughts of that suspect impair your ability to look at the rest of the evidence objectively. If you are not collecting evidence, you should evaluate any biases you may have which could affect your ability to be objective throughout the entire investigation. This can also tie into evidence gathered by witnesses. If you are unsure of the witness's ability to be objective, you should not disregard their contribution, but you should always consider what role their emotions may play.

We have gone over quite a few specific examples of how to use critical thinking in your everyday life. The following will discuss specific professions that utilize critical thinking and other aspects of life where you use critical thinking. This could be useful if reading this helped solidify your critical thinking skills, and you are looking for a profession that will allow you to use your newfound skill. This part can also be useful if you're looking to work on your new skill with practical examples. Through the examples, you can use them to identify evidence, create questions, answer questions, and solve problems methodically.

Thinking Critically in Your Career

The first career that comes to mind is an *investigator*, partly because it has been a part of many of the examples used in this book and partly because critical thinking is investigating. This is a skill necessary for all investigators because coming to the correct conclusion can be life-changing for an individual. On the extreme side of things, if someone is wrongly convicted of murder, it would be because of a mistake the investigator made in their critical thinking process.

Any type of *educator* needs to be able to think critically. If they are not efficient thinkers, they cannot teach other people how to think critically. They are also required to develop lesson plans and answer questions to determine how each student learns best. They need to be able to look ahead in time to determine the pace the class needs to work at. They will also need to draw conclusions about the best methods to teach a variety of topics.

As a *doctor or nurse*, critical thinking is imperative. A wrong decision can be the difference between life and death. To make a diagnosis, a doctor must assess a patient's symptoms – which will be considered evidence – and use deductive reasoning to come to a conclusion and create a treatment plan. Nurses must react quickly and be efficient. They must be able to understand each patient they deal with and must remain emotionally detached.

Any type of *manager* must understand how to settle disputes, create a schedule that works for everyone, and maintain a happy work environment. This can be difficult when dealing with a broad variety of people. This requires divergent thinking, creativity, and being a strong leader.

These are a few examples. You could go through hundreds of careers and make a case for why critical thinking is required in that field of work. The point is, critical thinking is important and necessary in today's day and age. If you are unwilling to train your brain to think critically, success will be further from your reach. Critical thinking is so important that most schools are requiring it to be inserted into the curriculum. By creating more critical thinkers, productivity will be higher. Cures to diseases will be found, and we will begin living greener. Critical thinking may seem simple in the grand scheme of things, but it is more important than you know. Develop your critical thinking skills now to impress in the future.

Chapter 6: Ways to Think More Critically

This section will provide a few strategies to help you think critically. You do not need to think critically about every decision you make, even if you could. However, doing this would take up more time than the days allow. Try to keep critical thinking outside of places like the grocery store, the gym, and your mind when you are trying to sleep. We know that sleep deprivation can affect your ability to make decisions!

Anyway, these strategies will help you when you are going to college, writing a paper, or buying a house.

Ask Questions

You may get lost when you are trying to think critically. You may ask so many questions that you don't even know what questions you asked originally. It's like the black hole of critical thinking. This can be exhausting and discouraging. But don't stop! Go back to the basic questions and write it all down. If you write it down, the paper will remember for you.

Remember, brain capacity is limited. (If you remember anything, remember that.) Asking basic questions first is also important because not every question has a complicated answer. Sometimes, you won't even need to go through the critical thinking process to find your solution. This will save you time and energy (and a little brain capacity).

Questioning Basic Assumption Leads To Innovation

In the beginning, we assumed the Earth was flat until someone decided to stop assuming that. Now we know it is round. Just because something was never proven false does not mean it is true. We have talked so much about how we can't always make assumptions. Therefore, let's break the habit! Who knows what you might discover for us next.

Be Aware Of Your Mental Processes

Self-awareness, self-awareness, self-awareness! Being aware of your own thought process is important, especially since it moves so quickly. Keep those cognitive biases in mind!

Work Backward

Sometimes, if you find yourself stuck, you can flip things around to get to the answer. You may think it is obvious that X caused Y, but it's entirely possible that Y caused X. Now, ask yourself what came first, the chicken or the egg?

Form Your Own Opinions

Even if you are wrong, they can give you a good starting point. This is kind of like the thesis statement of your paper. It helps you decide what you are trying to prove but can be totally different by the time you finish your paper because of the evidence you found.

Conclusion

Thank you for making it through to the end of *Critical Thinking: How to Improve Your Critical Thinking and Problem-Solving Skills and Avoid The 25 Cognitive Biases in Decision-Making*. Let's hope it was informative and able to provide you with the skills to find the answers to all of your problems, whether they may be big or small.

Just because you have finished this book doesn't mean there is nothing left for you to learn on the topic. Expanding your horizons is the only way to find the mastery you seek. I have stated several times that there are hundreds of sources out there just waiting for you to dive in.

The next step is to stop reading and write that paper or solve that problem. Remember that you shouldn't abandon learning about critical thinking. You do use it in your everyday life, after all. If you find that you still need help getting started, return to the model that this guide utilized. Start by thinking in simple terms and expand upon it. Make the switch from thinking convergently to divergently. Practice your critical thinking skills next time you are tuning into an episode of *Law and Order*.

Be conscious of the critical thinking process when you are writing. Thinking critically about your writing can help you in a number of ways which you learned. You must be able to write clearly and concisely in order for your argument to be considered usable by others. You must be able to eliminate cognitive biases to strengthen your arguments. Use this book if you are on the debate team or in a speech communication class. This is a way to enhance the learning process.

Utilize all of the strategies that this book has taught you. You have learned how to think like a lawyer, and after this, you will be a problem-solving pro.

Next time you are working in a group, think about the effects of Groupthink and urge your group to use some of the strategies we talked about and see how well your team will start performing for yourself. In addition, turn identifying biases into a game and then work to eliminate them with your team. This will increase productivity and empathy throughout.

Remember how important asking questions is and never hesitate if you are looking for answers. Take time to weigh big decisions and decide what they're worth. Making the wrong choice because you did not take the time to think it through is the worst possible outcome. Don't forget that you will use critical thinking in your place of work, in your home, while you are driving, and while you're writing papers. Refer back to the examples and exercises this guide has provided you with to find more success in your life. Furthermore, don't let your inability to think critically hold you back. Practice it so that you won't lose it.

Lastly, if you found this book useful in any way, recommend it to your friends and don't forget – a review on Amazon is always appreciated!

Check out more books by Scott Lovell

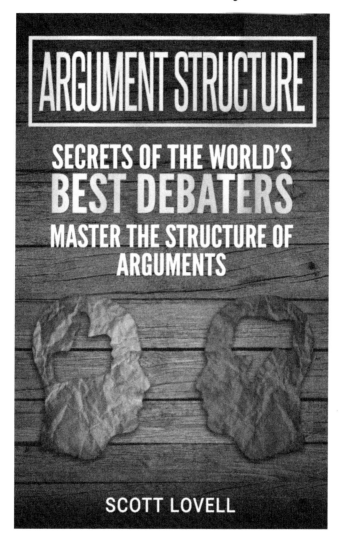